AFTER EDEN

ALSO BY
DIANE VREULS

Instructions
Are We There Yet?
Let Us Know
Sums: A Looking Game

After Eden

POEMS BY
DIANE VREULS

PINYON PUBLISHING

Montrose, Colorado

Copyright © 2015 by Diane Vreuls

Cover Art by Elizaveta Buinosova

Photograph of Diane Vreuls by Joan Stephenson

Design by Susan Elliott

First Edition: November 2015

Pinyon Publishing
23847 V66 Trail, Montrose, CO 81403
www.pinyon-publishing.com

Library of Congress Control Number: 2015953570
ISBN: 978-1-936671-34-2

Acknowledgments

Grateful acknowledgment is made to the following publications in which some of these poems first appeared or are forthcoming:

AFCU Journal: "Christina the Astonishing" and "Holy Week"

America: "Mary of Sorrows" and "L'Heure Bleue"

ARTS: "Death Does Not Compare"

Cloudbank: "Late Spring"

Commonweal: "Adorations," "Anno Animae in Terra," "Roll Call Fourth Grade" ("Annunciations" Part 5), "Healing," "He Came a Baby," "Thirst," "Valley," and "Which"

Lalitamba: "Directions"

Pinyon Review: "Annunciations"

Spiritus: "After Eden"

Weavings: "The Wink."

"January" was first published in *The Chariton Review* 36/2 (Fall 2013).

"Here to Where" and "Pilgrimage" originally appeared in *Christianity and Literature*. Reprinted with permission.

In addition, several poems appeared in *Instructions*, from Kayak Books.

I would like to thank Sr. Mary Ann Flannery, S.C., for her encouragement, and the Jesuit Retreat House of Parma, Ohio, for physical and spiritual nourishment.

And most of all

Stuart

without whom ...

CONTENTS

I THE FIRST WORD

If	3
Annunciations	4
Advent	8
He Came a Baby	9
Holy Week	10
Botanicon	12

II THE LONG SILENCE

After Eden	15
To Receive My Speech	16

III LONGING TO BELIEVE

Who	27
Valley	28
Late Spring	29
Pilgrimage	31
Directions	34
Temple	36

Small Altars   37
Morning Mass   39
Thirst   40
Cure   41
Elsewhere   42
Which   43
Death Does Not Compare   44
Song   45
Do Not   46

IV   THE GRIEF OF OTHERS

Adorations   49
Mary of Sorrows   51
Saint Sourise   52
Saint Perpetua   54
Christina The Astonishing   55
Delia   56
Malcolm   57
The Wink   59
Healing   60
Physic   61

V INTO OR OUT OF

January	65
Here to Where	66
Knowledge	70
Source	71
A Prayer to the Gardener	72
L'Heure Bleue	73
White	74
Post Partum	75
Anno Animae in Terra 2015	76

I

THE
FIRST
WORD

I F

I
learn
English
the
first
word
will
be
You.

ANNUNCIATIONS

1

Was it a dove
or the thought of a dove
broke my sleep?

Later, the voice
just behind the ear.
No matter how fast you turn your head,
a throb of silence.

Then something neither memory nor dream.

2

Is the message new or old?

3

Mary told Elizabeth told Joanna told Sylvia told
(Mouth to ear, mouth to ear) Anna told Margaret
told
        Is what I hear
        what was said?

Was it my name?

4

You can watch for hours and not grow weary.
You can stroke and touch and not grow numb,
but to lie long in wait for a sound will deafen the spirit.
Only animals have the skill
to detect the icy click of branch against branch
then listen one whole season
for the faint release of water's flow.

Except ye come young.

5

Roll call fourth grade.
Philip Jesperson didn't recognize his name.
Philip Bade wouldn't take his seat.
Betsy answered only to Elsabeth Ann.
Susan wept in the cloakroom.
"Here" was the only word we ever heard from Tom.
Roger came late, was punished daily.
Diane was sick a lot.
Someone we didn't know never came at all.

Later we learned Roger walked three miles. Susan was beaten.
Philip B. was hard of hearing. Philip J. never grew beyond
fourth grade. Who didn't come? Gypsy children camped at
Dam Number 4. Isa working in the family bakery. And Mary.
That was the year the Virgin Mary appeared in vacant lots all
over America. She never came to Illinois.

6

Did Gabriel call on many women who refused?
Those who refused to be overpowered? To conceive?

7

She was on her way to the well to draw water,
gathering herbs, or perhaps she was watching
the village children or stirring the soup in her family's dwelling
when she was visited by an angel. I don't think it was at night.
She was not sleeping. She was afraid, but spoke up smartly.
How can this be? It is.

8

With every breath the Holy Spirit calls us into being
as that breath forms our names.
Again and again, the breaths, our names.
Presente.

9

Who is the being of light embracing
behind me always, the way the moon
lights the clouds that would cover it,
the way the streambed gleams through the water,
the way the power pronounces the word.
What is this singing, this singing so high it is painful,
and will not be silenced?

10

Aren't all children conceived by the Holy Spirit?
Isn't every birth an Emmanuel?

11

So many questions.

Annunciation is a question.

Let the answer be yes.

ADVENT

To get ready for a baby
1. Clean house.
2. Put away all dangerous objects.
3. Make a soft bed in a warm place,
like your heart.

HE CAME A BABY

To take on flesh,
    hunger and thirst.
        To learn pain.

Born without words
    the Word, where angels sang
        his cry rose in the midnight air.

He had to learn to trust us
    to feed him, give him drink,
        teach him to speak and walk.

And fed, he preached
    and walked the long walk
        to the cross

and drank the cup.
    His cry to heaven
        hung in the air

until he spoke forgiving words
    and swaddled in his grave
        left us, newborn.

HOLY WEEK

Palm Sunday
In our hands
as we read the Passion
the palm becomes a whip
a sword
a lance.

Tenebrae
When the lights are restored
it is still dark.

Maundy
When the host
leaves the banquet
don't mourn.
It is not our last supper
with Christ.

Friday
Someone
somewhere else
is put to death this day
who cannot be as innocent as you, Lord,
yet you were just as dead as he.

Holy Saturday
We wait.

Easter
We gaze at the altar flowers.
Christ gazes at the flowers.
We meet.
The unseen appearing.
The hoped for
here.

BOTANICON

Each March
the earth
sends forth
fresh shoots
of bush and tree
not pale
firstlings
of green growth
but wine-
red tendrils
carmine whips
a blush
of buds
burst from
earth's blood
announcing
Resurrection.

11

THE
LONG
SILENCE

AFTER EDEN

Wind
out
of
compass
bird
out
of
speech
flowers
that
have
bloomed
in
no
tongue
before,
what
do
I
name
you
how
shall
I
call
you
what
are
your
fruits
after
Eden
O
Lord?

TO RECEIVE MY SPEECH

1

When I broke my flutes,
Pierced my drums,
Cut the strings of my rib harp

When from long dryness
The sounding bowl cracked,
Releasing its silence

You did sing through me, Lord.
On the breath of my breath
You did sing.

2

(chip and seal)

On the Jericho Road
I don't ask who gathers the crowds
in passing, don't pause, gawk,
beg—even once—for mercy.
Against street hosannas, gutter miracles,
I turn my back,
strike a new route home.
Your voice calling after me
sounds like tires screeching.

16

Once in late winter,
crossing College Street
on the way home after classes,
that same screech of tires
but no car in sight,
nothing that moved,
just a dog splayed in the road,
making over and over the sound
of the object that struck him.

3

If faith comes through the ear
The devout deaf are our most holy.

4

At the Elmwood Place Friends Meeting
in the former kindergarten building
hunched in child chairs around a flowered rug
our weekly silence was unbroken
until the Sunday a professor of American
Transcendentalism (retired) stopped by
to deliver himself of a few words they
hadn't wanted to hear at the Universalist-
Unitarian meeting across town.

We listened.

Thereafter week upon week, as he stood and roared
the text God dictated to him the night before
for our enlightenment, what could we do but listen?

Birthright Quakers took him aside. Promptings,
they said, are spontaneous; leadings rarely given.
The inner light, they said.

His gaze was blinding; his volume doubled.

Again they took him aside.

Again he thundered, as he said,
from the headwaters of eternity.
Only John spoke from such wilderness, brooked
such Jordans: this was preaching!

I left the meeting.

5

Walking down Peterson
before it was paved, just a cinder path
through Illinois prairie, flat,
iced with sunset

and cold.
Last bus from highschool
emptied of me, all that moved
in that landscape

now gone.
Boots on cinders, breaking
through shallow ice ponds,
bearing into wind

so raw I was stripped to
destination:
Courtland to Prospect,
Prospect to Fairview,

heading into a western sky
so dark—though it was only five—
that its single crimson stripe
was an astonishment,

heading homeward, gazing
anywhere but forward, I
counted weeds stuck frozen
in the fields, looked for late geese

to mount the sky or planes from Douglas
Aircraft to land across the silence, or
the hunger moon to catch the rack
of roiling clouds, and spill its
light into my way—And was instead

caught upward, arced
into a realm I can't speak of even now,
sixty years down that same road
unpaved, frozen,
absolute.

6

From too long listening, deliver us.

A weed sows a forest
and every leaf's a tongue
and every blade of corn, of grass, a tongue,
and every tongue of every creature
a tolling.
    Houses tower
    towers babel
    and from the windows people lean and shout:
I—I am the news!
And the newscasters are
the books and records are
the mall and mailed and unmailed
documents and diaries
speaking
    and the miked stars
    and the sonogrammed blood
    amps the music of the spheres
and through this You
are speaking too.
    Too many speakers
story upon story
and all I heard was truth.

And too much truth becomes, at last, a lie.

And the ears shut, then the throat,
and I entered the long silence.

7

It's a bad sleep,
the dream you tell yourself is just a dream,
an obligation you won't remember.
It is refusing to say the one thing
that would ease another's heart.

It is eating without fill.
An unanswered door.

Like the child's tower of blocks
that is not finished until it topples,
the long silence builds and crashes
builds and crashes
and nothing to show for it
but a tired child.

8

What is the animal that sleeps standing up?

No, the one that sleeps standing on books,
counting to ten in five
foreign languages, uno zwei tri quattro cinq,
though she sees from her stall but three trees
and no stars.

9

St. Hilda, about to sail to France,
to "live a stranger for our Lord" (says Bede)
was stopped by Bishop Aidan and given land
on the north side of the River Wear,
where for a year she lived as a monastic,
with few companions, before being made an abbess,
first at Heruteu, then at Whitby, where Caedmon sang.

So did I hope that when God struck me down
in the road—it was four in the afternoon
at the northwest corner of Main and Vine, '81,
when I found myself slammed to the pavement
by the flat of God's hand—
so did I think when he raised me up, set me
here to stay, it would be preparation.
And so it was—
for yet a longer stay, and here.

　　　　　And God gave
　　　　　and I did not receive.

I am not a dog in the road that you should feed me.

　　　　　And God gave.

10

Begging by the Jericho Road,
the blind man heard the feet of people running.
"What is happening?" he asked.
"The Nazarene is passing," they told him.
And he shouted, "Son of David, have mercy!"
"Be quiet!" hissed the people.
But the beggar shouted louder than before,
"Son of David, have mercy on me!"
Jesus stopped, drew the man before him, and said,
"What do you want me to do?"
"Lord," I said, "teach me to ask."

11

How is it we wake?
Without bells,
The blare of trumpets,
What rouses us?

Something we hear in our sleep
Then forget at once,
Like the song that dies in our ears
The moment we're born.

When from long silence
The sounding bowl cracked,
When I finally asked
For that song back

You did sing through me, Lord.
On the breath of my breath
You did sing.

III

Longing
To
Believe

WHO

If
you
are
speaking
the
same
word
I
am
speaking,
who
is
speaking
us?

VALLEY

Your opponent the devil is prowling ...
—1 Peter

Near the stone ledge
where I sleep
the lion paces.
All night
he walks back and forth above me,
then leaps to the ledge,
settles in close.
I feel the heat of his flanks,
the brush of his breath
as he studies my face,
thinking it over,
thinking it over.

LATE SPRING

Cycling past a farmer's field
sided by staunch trees
invaded by sunlight, I watch
turkey buzzards circle and dive
into the furrows, come up crying.
In the shade of a far acre
a combine rusts among young weeds—
mustard and wild geranium
and flowers I can no longer name.

This is a spring in my waning years
but still a spring, still a beginning.
As I ride slowly past this field,
row after planted row fans open
and reveals a passage I can see almost
to its end before I pedal by and it closes,
just as a loved one found in a dream
is lost at waking, or a glimpse of memory
dissolves upon recognition.

And I recall what has been unresolved
and keeps me dreaming, working for resolution
before I wake: the search for the missing trunk,
the lost address, the room in which I must give
the lecture or take the test, the house we sold,
the way to the foreign city where we lead
a parallel life of obligation.

Clouds change the sky
the way each moment alters my history
and promises a wiping clean, an absolution
not of night failures, but of the daylight sins they
mimic and obscure. What was carelessly lost.
What was not cherished enough. What I had
failed to be tested by. I try to pedal past
but the wind at my back shifts suddenly,
takes my breath, stops me in the road.

I don't know where I am.
I don't know the way forward
nor the way back, only that I am here,
and the road endures.
The road endures.

PILGRIMAGE

No traveler, not even fools, shall go astray.
—Isaiah

1

On our tour of Teresa's foundations
some convents were shuttered and locked.
We rang portal bells and shouted
but not even pigeons were roused.
We idled in unshaded streets
stared at chalky walls, took hot strolls
or sat back on our heels while our guide
phoned someone who didn't answer
and the driver slipped off for a drink.
An occasional dog snarled for snacks,
cats bedded under our bus.
No one else appeared on the pavement:
the silence was penitential.
Did Teresa's nuns take siestas?
We couldn't remember her regimen,
but rest in the Lord, why not?
Why were we clamoring at the gate?
It was clear we'd come 4,000 miles
to learn to wait.

2

The English couple at Taizé
asked for addresses of U.S. retreats
offering travel stipends for foreign seekers.
They'd done Lourdes, Fatima, Loreto,

Santarem, Medjugorje,
sampled El Camino by bus. Croagh Patrick
was too steep, the inn at St. Winefride's Well
too dear, but surely there were low-cost
cures to be had in my country? I thought of
the healing mud of Chimayó, of the pilgrims,
some hiking a hundred miles
along freeways, up dusty desert roads
in the sun, walking every day of Holy Week
shouldering crosses, carrying flowers
to the shrine to ask for God's mercy,
freely given.

3

A striped cat ran up the 100 steps
of St. Joseph's Oratory in Montreal,
past the veiled women
mounting the stairs on their knees,
past the climbers chanting their beads,
past the verger who opened
the large oaken door
for a man in a wheelchair,
women on crutches,
past the font, the windows, the pews,
headed straight up the nave
toward the altar, then disappeared.
Some say the devil caught it by
the tail, some think it's catching mice
in the cellar, I say it's curled up on
that stature of Mary, warming her lap
for the Child.

4

In a small bay on Loon Lake
there's a tree with a hole in the trunk
the shape of an owl.
Each time I canoed to the bay
after the long push up the shore,
I'd lie back and slowly float
over half-sunken logs through lily pads
straight to the tree and its empty hole.
One afternoon I heard hooting there,
but it was just a fooling wind.

Our last summer at the lake I paddled
to all my best places. The bank of wild
blueberries, the watery field of pickerelweed
where bears fished and dragonflies
rode my oars, the steep cliffs
where eagles taught their young to fly,
and last of all, the tree.

I entered the bay in a soft rain,
paddled quickly to the far shore,
and there in the hole in the tree—
no owl, but a nest. And nearby,
a rustle, a flash of wing,
something waiting for me to leave,
waiting for what would be born.

DIRECTIONS

To find the way you have to know the way.

*

To arrive at the temple gate you stop at an inn,
hear voices, the ring of pots in an inner room
and wait.

*

When no one comes
you join two travelers passing on the road.
They turn up a mossy path, climb through pines
past the sound of water that is not rain,
the tock of wood striking wood,
and bells shaking the branches.
Stones piled on stones and lanterns line the path.
They may be shrines, or only stones.

*

Speaking in their language,
small winds busy the firs.

*

The ascent steepens.
We have lost sight of the travelers.

*

In the clearing we find
no building,
no shrine,
only ourselves emerging.

*

Have we lost our way?
Or found
the temple?

TEMPLE

The house
I carry
within me.
The room
of the house
I carry
within me.
The altar
of the room.
You the flame
the candle
the table
the room
of the house
I enter.
Or do we enter
together
to find we have
always
been there?

SMALL ALTARS

Laps
plates
palms
sighs
the patch
of grass
by the highway
cross, the silence
before prayer.

Offer up
bone's ache
cruel questions
memory's pain
debts unpaid
sins you do not know
how to name.

Offer now
a snatch of song
your mother sang
white barns
in darkened fields
absent face
air of long-awaited
rain.

Gather then
all that's given
into the lap
the palm
the plate,
and as you travel
cross-lined roads
let your sighs
let your silence
be prayer.

MORNING MASS

My times are in your hand

They said it was only a while
I would have to be gone.
They said they couldn't come with.
Then they dropped me into the dark,
down, down, and alone,
the soul's first journey.
I remember how they were merry,
the birthing band, how well they willed me,
gave me gifts. I remember the tremor
and shine of their voices, the circle clothing me
with their voices, and in the sending,
the small winds of their hands.

What is a while?
Time. By twelve I'd had my fill of it.
My mother had wept at twelve, she said,
because she had passed the age when the dead
become angels, so she might as well live.
They weren't angels that sent me here,
nor dead, and I wanted them back.

Circles within circles within circles.
Does this coiled life choke inward
or spring us into the next?
Or are we danced,
handed off from circle to circle
to come at last to a gathering like this
morning Mass

where, in the earliest light,
we do birth.

THIRST

The wine is sour
which we drink without a blessing
and dark, staining the cloth
that covers the table
which is not Christ.

You, new sweet drink,
You give us:
first, yourself;
and after, thirst.

CURE

Mark 8:24

After the first touch
I see people

but they look like reeds
swaying.

My eyelids burn.

You put Your hand to Your mouth.
You lay Your hand on my eyes.

When I open them
I see people walking toward me

And in each face
I see You.

ELSEWHERE

By moonlight
reminded of the moon
I turn my back on it
sleep.

At its setting
I wake
watch it slip down the window
into a bank of cloud
so slowly it's hard to know
the moment it has vanished.
Elsewhere, lit by sun
it rises.

So may we die,
welcomed into the light
of God's face.

WHICH

At the Fifth Station of the Cross
I am asked to "accept in particular
The death that is destined for me"
    Which I must keep myself from guessing
    Which I cannot refuse.

At the First Station of the Cross
I am asked to say to Jesus
"I love you more than I love myself"
    Which I long to believe.
    And which is already a dying.

DEATH DOES NOT COMPARE

The
single
bird
in the
total
air
shot
down
leaves
still
its space
of song.

SONG

Practice a crocus
to measure the snow
stars in daylight
cooking with nettles.
The postman buries
the mail. An accident
on the pavement,
the pine gone.

Someone you had loved
you love again.

When you learn
all the words
the song stops singing.

DO NOT

leave
the
ark
unless
you
know
a
gull
from
a
dove
in
the
blinding
rain.

IV

THE
GRIEF
OF
OTHERS

ADORATIONS

Adoration of the Magi from the Life of the Virgin: Dürer

A noisy scene:
Angel trio in the heavens
warbling and strumming,
two magi volubly disputing,
Joseph itching to join in,
and in the upper left
the star a firework
bursting into bloom.
But look below:
mother and child
lapped in silence.

Adoration of the Magi: Cristofano di Michele Martini Robetta

The sky is racked with scouring winds.
No one rejoices,
not the trumpeting angels
not the crowding courtiers
not Joseph, old and defeated
fixing his wife with a querulous look
which Mary will not answer
while the baby exchanges baleful glances with a bull.
Only two foreground figures seem happy.
Magi? Donors?
Foreigners for sure,
aware only of the child
and not of the natives,
not of the natives, and what they will do.

Adoration of the Child with a Portrait of the Donor: Lombard School

The cattle nose in, mildly interested.
Joseph leans on his staff,
in arthritic pain, perhaps, or grief.
Mary, in pink, is restored as a virgin,
waist girt tight, pale hands full of grace.
We don't know where the donor is looking,
but it is not at the baby lying naked on the ground,
Mary's dark cloak spread beneath him,
his halo barely glistening, streaked with thorns.

MARY OF SORROWS

—for CM

We do not in our country
niche you at corners,
crossroads, highway shrines.
But in Karen's face as she talks of her son
whose pain will not redeem the world;
as Marguerita, whose eldest will not
survive her; in Sylvie, whose child
learned all his letters in his second year
and by age four had been condemned
to mute incomprehension,
you appear.

Son-bearer,
mother of mothers,
we know we cannot be spared;
help us bear our sorrows
and the sorrows of our children.
Help us bear.

SAINT SOURISE

1

The night she heard the cries of a man being tortured
two countries distant, she prayed for the one
who awakened her, then for the torturer.

2

Reclining after her midday meal she heard the cries
of the infant Jesus and ran to gather him close.
In the stall lay a newborn calf nosing the teat of its mother.

3

The cries of a woman in labor
gladden her heart. It is the sound,
she says, of the Earth birthing the day.

4

Come to the altar, she cries,
and you will hear your name whispered
in the pouring wine.

5

She is said to have died of grief—the grief
of others. If you wake in the night, she told us,
you have heard my cry.

SAINT PERPETUA

Put to death in Carthage in 203 A.D.,
leaving behind a husband and small baby.

Those whom life has martyred
honor you not. The motherlorn,
parents whose children died for a cause,
husbands whose wives self-sacrificed—
all who are losers' keepers tell you
God did not require you to die.

Some sit on columns, fast on wafers,
rush into the arena. It starts
with a small renunciation,
a quick vow, an hour at prayer—
but once a gift of self is given,
the heart, stirred to desire, cries *more*.
And so these lovers race
the reckless road to sainthood,
losing all they had but God.

Is there more to say?
That God is All?
That everything not God
shall pass away
or pass into divinity
with everyone we mourn
and those who mourned you,
Saint Perpetua?
That your name will live
to witness at least this:
That only God can know
what is a cry of pain,
and what a song.

CHRISTINA THE ASTONISHING

returned from the dead
to save the poor souls she'd seen
in Purgatory.

It is said she
hid in ovens, climbed trees,
flew up like a bird
to the rafters of a church
to escape the intolerable smell
of human beings.

Seven centuries on
I, no saint, have climbed trees,
hid in the rafters of barns,
camped in my study,
my kitchen, my church, seeking
separation more than solitude.

Now growing old,
I long for those I've shunned,
Seek their touch and, yes, their smell,
lest I too go to the dead
and not know the scent of Your pungent
earth, and those made from its clay
in Your image.

DELIA

Said she couldn't die because they might make
a mistake and send her to heaven and she'd
have to face her mother and she'd been a bad girl.

Said she was sorry she'd been bad and could I read her
the psalms and pray for her soul and please turn up the heat in
this freezing room and stop the oxygen from drowning her.

Wanted to know how David could write down his songs in a
sheep meadow. Didn't want me to read *Who can live and not see*
death? Who can save himself from the power of the grave?

Said the pain was bad now but her mother's anger
was worse, how she'd struck her when she came back late
and laughing, how she'd made her turn against

the only boy who ever loved her, stop their baby.
But don't make me talk about that time, I need an ice pack
and another blanket, and after that I didn't care what I did.

But if the baby is in limbo, how can I get there?
And now they say there is no limbo so where do they put
babies? Did David have children? What did he sing to them?

Read me those psalms. The pain is worse now.
Does it burn away the memory of her sins?
She won't say: her psalm is silence.

MALCOLM

He doesn't greet you, just amps up
the conversation playing in his head.
He thinks "so long" means much too long
and tries to keep you near
with secret information he's been sent.
Wave goodbye, he thinks it means stop
so he sits down on the grass and will not move
until a housemate comes to fetch him in.

They said he would never learn to read
but he reads everything he touches
with blunted fingers and lifts
to his ears, including dandelions
and the hands of strangers who,
when he reaches out to hug them,
try to push him away.

Malcolm has a giant trike
with a tall yellow pennant at the rear.
He rides it down the sidewalks of our town
proud as an admiral at the wheel.
In his basket is an old transistor radio
he will show you if he thinks you are a friend.
It is the source of all his secrets
and tells him where to go and what to say
in the voice, he confides, of his mother.

Malcolm's group home is near our church.
One Sunday he burst in during Mass
and in his lurching gait he joined the line
for Eucharist. And when he reached the priest,
he cupped his hands to get what we were given.
Thanks be to God, for once in Malcolm's life
that's what he got.

THE WINK

—in memory JBV

She had to twist her mouth to shut one eye,
laughing at how she knew she looked,
hoped it was conspiratorial, sly.
She practiced all her life, perhaps,
for that one moment
sitting straight in her chair on the pavement
waiting for the medics to load her
into the hospice van.
In her robe, in that heat, in her pain,
she turned to me,
winked.

HEALING

Some procedures have no pain
that we remember.
Anesthetized, we slowly wake
to the delirium of daylight,
the gated bed, the tubes, telemetry,
the insistent recall to identity,
the life we are required to resume—
it is there pain takes up residence.
They call it healing.

My daughter, lifted from the cross,
must now endure recovery.
My neighbor, crawling from the grave,
must now walk upright.
Our soldiers, damaged in an instant,
must mend for years.

They say the suffering unto health
hurts less than suffering unto death.
Those suffering don't say this.

They say: We are broken, Lord,
like Communion bread.
What can we do but kneel
and open our hands?

PHYSIC

The eyes
of Christ:
coherent
light
cutting
exposing
healing
laser
of love.

V

INTO
OR
OUT
OF

JANUARY

White sun so low in the sky
shadows of distant windbreaks
darken the soy fields.
I follow a railway bed.
Old plow rows rise and fall,
petrified waves of an inland sea.
So rough the going, I walk a mile
eyes down, hunting the lesser tracks
that dart through the shrinking snow.
Where a culvert whistles a hidden wind
a small woods opens. Shells of acorns
and shagbark hickory crack underfoot.
I call this the Place of Hearing Birds, for they are
never seen. Dead branches clog
the path to a reservoir. Hand over hand
I climb the bank into a shock of cold.
The sun dazzles the platter of ice.
Overhead contrails streak, meteors in daylight,
and one two three four deer burst from a copse,
leap a creek, and vanish into bracken,
as much pursued as pursuing, but from what
to what, who can say? Or if on this early day
in a year so late in my life
I am walking into or out of these woods.

HERE TO WHERE

To the place where they go
the rivers keep on going.
　　　　　— Ecclesiastes

1

He always laced us up too tight,
headed down the river shouting
go fast or you'll catch on rocks,
rounded a bend into forest
and disappeared. We tried to follow,
my weak-ankled brother and I
who never overtook, found a log to sit on
and wait for his return. For us it's 1948, Illinois.
He's on a Dutch canal, young as we are now,
stronger and swift, hands clasped behind him,
head against the wind, our father,
head against the wind.

2

Straight-line winds
surge the courseways
break the riprap
one-hundred-year rains
top the levees
unheard the warnings
sirens too late
we mount the boat
row for Ararat.
Many years on
starburned, grizzle-eyed
boat full of fish and children
we hit shore.
It starts to rain.

3

Busman won't say what to pay.
Dollar? Shakes his head.
Not two. Not less.
Laughs on his wheel,
caroms down Franklin.
We twist and sway on the entry steps,
hang on hard,
never do get a seat,
never pay,
get there anyway.

4

The arroyos of the mind
once flowing fresh
fissure deep
with sudden rains.
Aging, I am remembering
thunderous heat,
the torrent of release
sweeping canyons
clean for the growth
of spring. Permit me, Lord,
in this violent season,
passage into the new.

5

God is an underground river,
says Meister Eckhart.
Yes, and the
forest pool and the sea
and the small cup of water
You hold out to me
as I walk toward You
never, I think, growing closer
but never farther away
than the sound of dew.

6

Body, my last home,
I leave
and journey south
losing stars
gaining stars,
eyes of the nightwind
watching shadows dry, recoil
into nebulas of dust.

I cannot wake from this,
so close to gone.

KNOWLEDGE

Won't someone call them off,
the answermen? Silence them,
these self-credentialed experts,
short-tempered, apodictic
jumping on and off high stools
on their carousels of inquiry
to answer questions we've never asked
on subjects long avoided.
Demanding gratitude and amazement,
they leave their castoff summations
in our unwilling hands.

To live long is to be burdened
with unwanted knowledge.
You try to resist it, forget it,
but the unwelcome has a sly way
of entry, and always overstays.

How about a second Eden
where the tree remains untouched,
the fruit untasted?
Where, free in our nakedness
we walk unshamed with God?

Or is this what death is for—
in that passage
from question to silence
a blessed release
from knowledge
to understanding.

SOURCE

Three
transfusions,

can't tell
whose
blood is
in my
veins,

but at
Eucharist
I know.

A PRAYER TO THE GARDENER

Some call them hearts-ease
or pensées. Pretty thoughts,
they wilt in the sun, these
pansies I plant every year
and hope are perennial. But
violets, their originals, bloom
on barren hillsides, in city lots,
gravel dumps, waste places,
surviving decades underfoot,
small, unattended, beautiful.

In your garden, O Lord,
let me be violet.

L'HEURE BLEUE

Hour of approach, hour of silence.
The brother sets down his axe in the woods.
The sister sets down her glasses on the table
and waits in the moment before prayer
that throbs from the tolling of the bell.
Shadows swallow shadows in the frigid air.

Hour of departure.
Ledgers toted, windows shuttered.
Late heading homeward, children
do not stop to play on the walk.
The wind stills, the sun
in the brief moment before it sets
catches a row of white houses in its flare.
From under the hedges, the heart of the firs,
darkness rises—the blue hour.

Time stops for breath, breathes.
Ovens are lit, then streetlamps, porches.
It starts to snow. It will snow all night.

WHITE

It is all
Epithalamium:
White
Incense
Rising
The wedding,
The birth,
The Easter Communion
At twelve
When I knelt at the rail
And was raised
Into the white garden
Of Christ.
When in my purest dress
Was given by Christ
To my man,
When in white sheets
I suckled my milk-
dazed child,
There were flowers,
Everywhere
White
Flowers.

I give them as witness
Take them as vows
They are the incense.
The lotus
The locus
Of consummation.

POST PARTUM

We thought You were careless,
stretched open Your hands
and let us drop through,

but this is not falling, not
drifting, but a widening
air, perceptibly lightening;

not a journey, but stasis,
a plenum You breathe in us,
Your breath. You hold us

for a perfect moment,
then release us. And we
cry our first cry

unto You.

ANNO ANIMAE IN TERRA 2015

So many years in time, my soul,
so long since I met you at the door
to this large plain room where all the children
looked up for a moment as we entered,
then turned again to their play.

How I have worn you thin with washings,
stretched you on the line to dry with winter winds
like my child's diapers, to freeze and shatter,
but you did not break. If the heart breaks
why do you not? A mystery of God.

In this place all is mystery.
In its hunger you are my bowl.
In its pain you measure music.
In its primer you read the first word—
the Yes I am trying to learn.

CPSIA information can be obtained at www.ICGtesting.com
Printed in the USA
BVOW02s1800151015

422574BV00001B/3/P

9 781936 671342